all year round

A BOOK TO BENEFIT CHILDREN IN NEED

ALL year

ROUND

A Book to Benefit Children in Need

Lisa Desimini
David Ricceri
Sara Schwartz
Dan Yaccarino

Scholastic Press
New York

every time someone buys this book, it will help a new school to open its doors, a job training program to graduate another class, a soup kitchen to serve another meal, a shelter to take in another family. The Robin Hood Foundation makes sure of that. A portion of the proceeds of this book will go to Robin Hood and, from there, to organizations doing the most to fight poverty. Robin Hood funds small, innovative non-profit groups that are doing wonders for children, teenagers, and their families. And your purchase will help them, all year round.

Snowmen, snowmen, ho-ho-ho men,
Big, round, smooth, and clean.
All the colors of the rainbow –
Red, yellow, blue, wintergreen.

We have a frosty party
With all of our friends,

There are snowflakes and icicles,
We hope it never ends!

Spring, spring, birds sing,
Seeds grow into flowers.

We all splash in muddy puddles
Made by gentle showers.

Bunnies, bears, and butterflies
are in a playful way.

Snowcaps melt on mountaintops,
Through longer, warmer days.

**Beaches beaches, no more teachers,
Summer's here at last!**

It's so hot you can't forget
To eat your ice cream fast!

So catch a wave and sing a tune,
And smile while summer's here.

Fall, fall, crows call,
As gray clouds roll by.

Cool winds blow autumn leaves
Across the crisp blue sky.

Scarecrows stand on golden hills,
And there they will remain,
Waiting for the seasons
To come around again.

Sara Schwartz

Lisa Desimini

HOW THIS BOOK CAME TO BE

Dan Yaccarino

The paint

David Ricceri

The mural

A SAFE PLACE TO LEAVE THEIR KIDS. That's what homeless women getting help in a drug and alcohol treatment program needed. And that's why Women In Need (WIN) turned to the Robin Hood Foundation.

WIN, a leading provider of housing and services to homeless women and their children, was moving its operations to a new headquarters when budget cuts hit, throwing a wrench into their plans for a fairy-tale-like child care center. So Robin Hood gathered a band of more than thirty companies to donate everything from diapers to baby food to high chairs.

After all the shelves were filled with picture books, the toy boxes were brimming with stuffed animals and finger paints, Robin Hood brought in four gifted children's book illustrators who volunteered to dress up the walls. It was their collective imagination that created the mural that led to this book. Over weekends and nights, Lisa Desimini, David Ricceri, Sara Schwartz, and Dan Yaccarino waved their magic brushes, inventing blue snowmen, giant pink birds, talking clouds, and dancing pumpkins—a seventy-foot celebration of the seasons. Looking at the mural, youngsters can almost jump in a pile of leaves or feel snowflakes land on their noses.

The fact that four artists donated their time and their talent to decorating the walls of a women's shelter made some headlines in New York. That's when Scholastic Press first heard about the project. Plans came together to make a book: artwork was scaled down and repainted, a poem was written, and, thanks to everyone's extraordinary efforts, *All Year Round* was made. Robin Hood funds WIN and one hundred other innovative non-profit organizations fighting poverty. As all of Robin Hood's administrative and fund-raising costs are underwritten, every penny donated to the foundation goes to those who need it most.

Money raised from the sales of this book will ensure that organizations like WIN continue their good work—winter, spring, summer, and fall.

— LONNI TANNER, ROBIN HOOD FOUNDATION